CAPE POETRY PAPERBACKS

ADRIAN MITCHELL
THE APEMAN COMETH

Adrian Mitchell
(and Apeman Mudgeon)

THE APEMAN COMETH

POEMS

JONATHAN CAPE
THIRTY BEDFORD SQUARE LONDON

FIRST PUBLISHED 1975
THIS PAPERBACK EDITION FIRST PUBLISHED 1975
© 1975 BY ADRIAN MITCHELL

JONATHAN CAPE LTD,
30 BEDFORD SQUARE, LONDON WC1

ISBN 0 224 01147 2

Acknowledgments . . . this is normally just a list of
magazines, but all my poems are performed at various
readings before being published. So my first
acknowledgment is to the people who've come to my
readings, secondly to *Green and Pleasant Land*,
Socialist Worker, the *Guardian, Iron, Beyond This
Horizon, Poems for Shakespeare, Worlds, Streetword,
Full House* and others who have published poems
in this book.

Printed in Great Britain by
Ebenezer Baylis & Son Ltd.
The Trinity Press, Worcester, and London.

Contents

Second burst

Dedication

This book is dedicated to my friends and allies, but especially my wife Celia and my children Alistair, Danny, Briony, Sasha and Beatrix.

'Let me say, at the risk of seeming ridiculous, that the
true revolutionary is guided by great feelings of love' —
Che Guevara.

In beauty   may I walk
All day long   may I walk
Through the returning seasons   may I walk
Beautifully will I possess again
Beautifully birds
Beautifully joyful birds
On the trail marked with pollen   may I walk
With grasshoppers about my feet   may I walk
With dew about my feet   may I walk
With beauty   may I walk
With beauty before me   may I walk
With beauty behind me   may I walk
With beauty above me   may I walk
With beauty all around me   may I walk
In old age, wandering on a trail of beauty,
                                    lively,   may I walk
In old age, wandering on a trail of beauty,
                                living again,   may I walk
It is finished in beauty
It is finished in beauty

- From the Navajo Night Way ceremony.

First burst

Bessie Smith in Yorkshire

As I looked over the billowing West Riding
A giant golden tractor tumbled over the horizon
The grass grew blue and the limestone turned to meat
For Bessie Smith was bumping in the driver's seat.

Threw myself down on the fertilised ground and cried:
'When I was a foetus I loved you, and I love you
                        now you've died.'
She was bleeding beauty from her wounds in the Lands
                           of Wrong
But she kept on travelling and she spent all her breathing
                           on song.

I was malleted into the earth as tight as a gate-post
She carried so much life I felt like the ghost of a ghost
She's the river that runs straight uphill
Hers is the voice brings my brain to a standstill

Black tracking wheels
Roll around the planet
Seeds of the blues
Bust through the concrete

My pale feet fumble along
The footpaths of her midnight empire

The Castaways or Vote for Caliban

The Pacific Ocean —
A blue demi-globe.
Islands like punctuation marks.

A cruising airliner,
Passengers unwrapping pats of butter.
A hurricane arises,
Tosses the plane into the sea.

Five of them, flung on to an island beach,
Survived.
Tom the reporter.
Susan the botanist.
Jim the high-jump champion.
Bill the carpenter.
Mary the eccentric widow.

Tom the reporter sniffed out a stream of drinkable water.
Susan the botanist identified a banana tree.
Jim the high-jump champion jumped up and down and
                          gave them each a bunch.
Bill the carpenter knocked up a table for their banana
                                        supper.
Mary the eccentric widow buried the banana skins,
But only after they had asked her twice.
They all gathered sticks and lit a fire.
There was an incredible sunset.

Next morning they held a committee meeting.
Tom, Susan, Jim and Bill
Voted to make the best of things.
Mary, the eccentric widow, abstained.

Tom the reporter killed several dozen wild pigs.
He tanned their skins into parchment
And printed the Island News with the ink of squids.

Susan the botanist developed new strains of banana
Which tasted of chocolate, beefsteak, peanut butter,
Chicken and bootpolish.

Jim the high-jump champion organized organized games
Which he always won easily.

Bill the carpenter constructed a wooden water wheel
And converted the water's energy into electricity.
Using iron ore from the hills, he constructed lampposts.

They all worried about Mary, the eccentric widow,
Her lack of confidence and her —
But there wasn't time to coddle her.

The volcano erupted, but they dug a trench
And diverted the lava into the sea
Where it formed a spectacular pier.
They were attacked by pirates but defeated them
With bamboo bazookas firing
Sea-urchins packed with home-made nitro-glycerine.
They gave the cannibals a dose of their own medicine
And survived an earthquake thanks to their skill in
jumping.

Tom had been a court reporter
So he became the magistrate and solved disputes.
Susan the Botanist established
A university which also served as a museum.
Jim the high-jump champion
Was put in charge of law-enforcement —
Jumped on them when they were bad.
Bill the carpenter built himself a church,
Preached there every Sunday.

But Mary the eccentric widow . . .
Each evening she wandered down the island's main
street,

Past the Stock Exchange, the Houses of Parliament,
The prison and the arsenal.

12

Past the Prospero Souvenir Shop,
Past the Robert Louis Stevenson Movie Studios,
Past the Daniel Defoe Motel
She nervously wandered and sat on the end of the pier
                                    of lava,
Breathing heavily,
As if at a loss,
As if at a lover,
She opened her eyes wide
To the usual incredible sunset.

Out

when I broke the light bulb an orange dropped out
when I peeled the orange a rabbit jumped out
when I shook the rabbit a parcel dropped out
when I opened the parcel your house fell out
when I rang the doorbell you were out

A Girl called Music

A girl called Music
She drifts where she's not allowed.
She can do a soft-shoe-shuffle
On an illuminated cloud.
She's the imaginary milkmaid
To the snorers in city attics.
Her eye is the porthole of the washing machine
In which a coat of many colours does acrobatics —

   She makes the bread rise
   And the Sun go sideways
   My tender submarine
   Adores her tideways —

Ten Ways to Avoid Lending
Your Wheelbarrow to Anybody

1 PATRIOTIC

May I borrow your wheelbarrow?
I didn't lay down my life in World War II
so that you could borrow my wheelbarrow.

2 SNOBBISH

May I borrow your wheelbarrow?
Unfortunately Lord Goodman is using it.

3 OVERWEENING

May I borrow your wheelbarrow?
It is too mighty a conveyance to be wielded
by any mortal save myself.

4 PIOUS

May I borrow your wheelbarrow?
My wheelbarrow is reserved for religious ceremonies.

5 MELODRAMATIC

May I borrow your wheelbarrow?
I would sooner be broken on its wheel
and buried in its barrow

6 PATHETIC

May I borrow your wheelbarrow?
I am dying of schizophrenia
and all you can talk about is wheelbarrows.

7 DEFENSIVE

May I borrow your wheelbarrow?
Do you think I'm made of wheelbarrows?

8 SINISTER

May I borrow your wheelbarrow?
It is full of blood.

9 LECHEROUS

May I borrow your wheelbarrow?
Only if I can fuck your wife in it.

10 PHILOSOPHICAL

May I borrow your wheelbarrow?
What is a wheelbarrow?

Saw it in the Papers

I will not say her name
Because I believe she hates her name.

But there was this woman who lived in Yorkshire.

Her baby was two years old.
She left him, strapped in his pram, in the kitchen.
She went out.
She stayed with friends.
She went out drinking.

The baby was hungry.
Nobody came.
The baby cried.
Nobody came.
The baby tore at the upholstery of his pram.
Nobody came.

She told the police:
'I thought the neighbours would hear him crying.
and report it to someone who would come
and take him away.'

Nobody came.

The baby died of hunger.

She said she'd arranged for a girl,
Whose name she couldn't remember,
To come and look after the baby
While she stayed with friends.
Nobody saw the girl.
Nobody came.

Her lawyer said there was no evidence
of mental instability.
But the man who promised to marry her
Went off with another woman.

And when he went off, this mother changed
from a mother who cared for her two-year-old baby
into a mother who did not seem to care at all.
There was no evidence of mental instability.

The Welfare Department spokesman said:
'I do not know of any plans for an inquiry.
We never became deeply involved.'
Nobody came.
There was no evidence of mental instability.

When she was given love
She gave love freely to her baby.
When love was torn away from her
she locked her love away.
It seemed that no one cared for her.
She seemed to stop caring.
Nobody came.
There was no evidence of mental instability.

Only love can unlock locked-up-love.

Manslaughter: She pleaded Guilty.
She was sentenced to be locked up
In prison for four years.

Is there any love in prisons?

She must have been in great pain.

Now she is locked up.
There is love in prisons,
But it is all locked up.

What she did to him was terrible.
There was no evidence of mental instability.
What we are doing to her is terrible.
There is no evidence of mental instability.

Millions of children starve, but not in England.
What we do not do for them is terrible.

Is England's love locked up in England?
There is no evidence of mental instability.

Only love can unlock locked-up love.

When I read about it in the papers I cried.
When my friend read about it in the papers he cried.
We shared our tears.
They did not help her at all.

She has been locked up
For locking up her love.
There was no evidence of mental instability.

Unlock all of your love.
You have enough to feed all those millions of children.
Unlock all of your love.
You have enough for this woman.

Cry if you like.
Do something if you can. You can.

Unlock your love and send it to this woman.
I am sending her my love.

A Spell to make a Bad Hour Pass

Unfold your hand
Place all of the bad minutes in a circle
In the palm of your hand

Close your fingers slowly
To form a gentle fist

Slowly turn your fist around
And let your eyes pass slowly
Over all the surface of your fist

Slowly turn your fist around
And let your lips pass slowly
Over all the surface of your fist

Slowly
Tighten your fingers
Slowly
Tighten your fist

The fist is clenched
All the bad minutes are inside it
The fist is clenched
This evil hour is vanishing

Slowly, slowly
Unfold the fingers of your hand

The palm of your hand is empty

Rest the back of your hand
Upon your other hand

Look into the palm of your hand
Look deep into your hand

Your hand is full
Your hand is full
Your hand is full of life

A Spell to make a Good Time Last

Walk with your lover through a doorway
Walk with your lover through the maytime sunlight
Walk with your lover by a lake

The past is a stone for playing ducks and drakes
The stone is lying at your feet
Skim the stone away across the lake

The future is a stone for playing ducks and drakes
The stone is lying at your feet
Skim the stone away across the lake

Lie down beside the water
Lie down beside your lover
Lie down beside the water
Lie down beside your lover

A Curse on my Former Bank Manager

May your computer twitch every time it remembers
                                        money
until the twitches mount and become a mechanical ache
and may the ache increase until the tapes begin to scream
and may the pus of data burst from its metal skin

and just before the downpour of molten aluminium
may you be preening in front of your computer
and may you be saying to your favourite millionaire
yes it cost nine hundred thousand but it repays every
                                        penny

and may the hundred-mile tape which records my debts
                                        spring out
like a supersonic two-dimensional boa-constrictor
and may it slip under your faultless collar and surround
                                        your hairless neck
and may it tighten and tighten until it has repaid every-
                                        thing I owe you

Jimmy Giuffre Plays 'The Easy Way'

A man plodding through blue-grass fields.
He's here to decide whether the grass needs mowing.
He sits on a mound and taps his feet on the deep earth.
He decides the grass doesn't need mowing for a while.

Love Note

when I know you're going away
I miss you before you've even gone
22

Statesman Stomp

Whenever a distinguished leader
Signs his treaty with death
And governments fly him frozen roses
And the press doesn't mention
That his breath was death.
When he's laid in state
With a lipstick job
And an aura of after-shave
And twenty-one guns have farted goodbye —
Dance on the bugger's grave.

Dance on the earth that's hotter than his life —
His blood was chilled.
Dance to the music of the human animals
The liar killed.

Stomp — 1, 2, 3, 4, 5, 6.
Stomp — 7, 8, 9, 10.
Stomp all night till the soil's right tight
So the bugger never rises again.

To the Silent Majority

ashamed to be white,
ashamed not to be in jail,
why do i keep howling about:

sky overcast with the colour of hunger,
liars who kiss like arsenic sandpaper,
white power gas, the torture game
and the one-eyed glare of that final global flame?

because they are here.

Ancestors

We had an island.
Oh we were a stomping old tribe on an island.
Red faces, hairy bodies.
Happy to be hairy
Happy to be hairy
When the breezes tickled
The hairs of our bodies
Happy to be hairy
Happy to be hairy
Next best thing to having feathers —
That was our national anthem.
Right. Hairy tribe,
Hairy red story-telling, song-singing, dragon-fighting,
                                        fire-drinking tribe.

Used to get invaded every other weekend.
Romans, Vikings, Celts — fire and sword —
Pushed us back but they never broke us down.
In between invasions we grew spuds and barley,
Took our animals wherever there was a river and some
                                        grass.

When the snows came, we moved south
When the rivers dried, we moved west
When the invaders came, we burnt our crops, moved.

Until one day we were surrounded by warriors,
The same old fire and sword, but used efficiently.
They slaughtered our warriors, lined up the rest of us
And there were speeches
About law and order, and firm but fair government.

And this is what they did,
This is government.
You take an island and cut it carefully
With the razorblade called law and order
Into a jigsaw of pieces.
The big, rich-coloured pieces

24

Go to the big, rich men.
The smaller, paler pieces,
(Five beds two recep barn mooring rights five acres)
Go to the small, rich men.
And nothing at all
Goes to those who have nothing at all.

Absurd? The many nothing-at alls
Wouldn't stand back and see their island
Slashed into ten thousand pieces.
They didn't stand back, our hairy tribal ancestors.
Some of them spoke out. Some fought back.
They were slashed down by the giant razorblade.

And now, and now the rich seldom have to kill
To defend the land they stole from all the tribe —
Wire fences. Guard Dogs Loose on these Premises.
                              No Trespassing.
Bailiffs. Security Guards. Police. Magistrates' Courts.
                              Judges. Prisons —
Grey prisons where the brain and the flesh turn grey
As the green English years stroll by outside the walls.
So who needs fire and sword?
The tribe has been tamed
And our island
Our daft green stony gentle rough amazing haven
Entirely surrounded by fish
Has been stolen from the tribe.
It was robbery with most bloody violence.
And that was history, history is about the dead.
Then is our tribe dead? Is our tribe dead?
Is the tribe dead?

Private Transport

round and round
his private roundabout
drives the little critic's car —
a sneer on four square wheels

Revolution

Its first shoots will burst out of the earth
silently, at the wrong time of year
in a silent part of the island
far from the patrolling armoured cars.

A finger, pointing towards the sun,
which will be mistaken for a blade of grass
if anybody notices it at all.

One deep night, an armoured division,
returning from an easy mission
in Leicester or in Birmingham
will be crushed by the branches
of the numberless, nameless trees
of an overnight forest.

And those breeding trees
with eccentric outlines
will be no more like our theories
than a hippopotamus
is like a parallelogram.

The Dichotomy Between the Collapse of Civilization and Making Bread

(To my students at Dartington)

No such thing as Western
civilization
No such thing as Eastern
civilization
The brand name for a tribe of killer apes
is civilization

The killer apes do some little good things
So let's all do the little good things
good things good and not many of them —
Coconuts in the pacific ocean
of bad things bad things calling themselves
civilization

What the hell if the tribe collapses
Look out look out for another tribe
of apes who do no killing but do big good things

Meanwhile look up
up above your head
only the rain is collapsing on you

Of course there's not much bread
in doing little good things
but do do do
altogether all the do do day

Because, speaking as a brother-speck
among the galaxies,
Little is the biggest we can call ourselves

The Apeman Cometh
chants and mutters
by
Apeman Mudgeon

Apeman keep thinking it's Wednesday

Woken up in fork of tree
By usual jungle jangle
No tom-toms.
No metal bird
Full of Nazi paratroops.
Jumped down
T H E L O N K!
Into turtle pool,
Splashed massive torso
Searched for berries with mate.
Ate berries with mate and young.
Groomed mate. Groomed by mate.
Groomed young.
Sent young to learn
Ways of jungle.
Bashed chest with fists,
Gave mighty howl,
Loped off into undergrowth to hunt.
Lay along thick branch,
Saw longhorned poem approaching.
Dropped on poem's back,
Grabbed its neck.
Big poem, threw me off.
Bump on head.
Tried liana swinging.
Good swinging.
Ninth liana bad liana,
Dropped me on rock.
Ankle go blue.
At water-hole discussed crocodiles
With seminar of chimpanzees.
Inspected poem-traps.
Only found one squeaky poem
Without a tail.
Too small, let it go.
Limped back to tree.
Told mate and young
About head and ankle.

Mate said she caught fish.
Ate fish with mate and young.
Fish taste like a good poem.
Sent young up trunk into tree.
Mated with mate.
Climbed up trunk.
Lay down in fork of tree.
Huge moon.
Dreamed about a poem stampede.

The Apeman who hated snakes

Was an apeman lived next door to me
In some kind of prickly tree.

That apeman had the angry shakes
Spending all his sleep in dreams about snakes.

And every morning he would shout
How all the snakes have to be stamp out.

Pastime he enjoy the best
Was to poke a stick down a mamba's nest

Or he'd have a slaughter down the old snake-pit
And look pretty happy at the end of it.

He tattooed snakes all over his skin
Coiling and hissing from knees to chin.

For breakfast he hard-boiled the eggs of snakes.
Suppertime — Boa-constrictor steaks.

For a man who hated reptiles so obsessively
He spend an awful lot of time in their company.

Now where that apeman lived next door to me
There's a vacancy in that prickly tree.

I reckon snakes are like me and you —
They got a mystery job to do.

So when I see one in my path I salute
And take a roundabout alternative route.

Apeman give a Poetry Reading

Apeman travel much in jungle
Sometimes he swing for many miles
To taxi down in some new clearing
No concert posters up on trees.
Tiger who arranged the gig
Has gone down with sabre-tooth-ache.
Gazelle apologises nervously.
Apeman and gazelle shift rocks around
To form a semi-circle.
Two or three crocodiles trundle in.
Four flying squirrels. One sloth.
Various reptiles and a fruit-bat.
Suddenly — ten-eleven multi-colour birds.
Apeman cheers up.
Gazelle checks time by the sun,
Introduces apeman.
Apeman performs a series
Of variegated apeman howls —
Comic howls, sad howls, angry-desperate howls.
Apeman runs out of howl, sits down.
Senior crocodile asks question:
What use is howling?
Howling does not change jungle.
Apeman stares at him,
Nods, shakes his head, gives up.
Animals begin to drift to holes and nests.
Apeman swings home heavily through the gloom.
If you meet apeman in this mood
Give him a hug.
Unless your name is Boa-constrictor.

The Apeman's Hairy Body Song

Happy to be hairy
Happy to be hairy
When the breezes tickle
The hairs of my body

Happy to be hairy
Happy to be hairy
Next best thing
To having feathers

The Apeman's Motives

He not hunt the poem for money —
The kind he catch fetch nowt.
He not hunt the poem for fun —
He not a very good sport.
Apeman go after poem
With fists and teeth and feet
Because he need the juices
Contained in the poem meat.

It Ain't what they do
it's what the Apeman do

What the gagmen do
the swagmen do
and the bagmen and the ragmen and the stagmen do

What the cashmen do
the bashmen do
and the flashmen and the crashmen and the moustachemen
do

do do do
altogether all the do do day
do do do
doing it the same old do do way

What the awful lawful
riflemen do
the shufflemen and trufflemen are doing it too

What the boo-hoo shoemen
and the bluemen do
the few human crewmen and bitumen men do

do do do
altogether all the do do day
do do do
doing it the same old do do way

But what the Apeman do
is what the Apeman do
except when he decides to do
something different from himself

The Apeman recollects emotions in tranqui
with a copy of the T. L. S. stuck up his arse

Jump that jungle
Jump that jungle
Pump that jungle
Pump that jungle
Eat that jungle
Eat that jungle
Heat that jungle
Heat that jungle
Joke that jungle
Joke that jungle
Soak that jungle
Soak that jungle
Sling that jungle
Sling that jungle
Sing that jungle
Sing that jungle
Grow that jungle
Grow that jungle
Blow that jungle
Blow that jungle
Make that jungle
Make that jungle
Shake that jungle
Shake that jungle
Climb that jungle
Climb that jungle
Chime that jungle
Chime that jungle
Plumb that jungle
Plumb that jungle
Come that jungle
Come that jungle
Shove that jungle
Shove that jungle
Love that jungle
Love that jungle
The jungle loves you

Apeman as Tourist Guide

Apeman show you round jungle?
All right.

Big cliff with holes in
Is baboon high-rise development.
Dusty clearing
With banyan tree full of honking birds
Is discotheque for elephants.
Quick! Jump in water — breathe through hollow reed —
Safari party of lions going by.

Tell you something:
Apeman love this
Hot and rowdy jungle.
Tell you something else:
Jungle not all like this.

You keep on walking
And soon or later
You will find the other jungle —

The frozen jungle,
Black ice
On every branch, tendril,
Pool, path, animal and man.

Black ice jungle
Where it's too cold
To see or hear
Too cold
To feel too cold to think
As heart and brains
Turn into black turn into ice.

Don't you worry.
Most of the jungle

Given over to
Sweaty celebration.
You may not stumble into
Black ice jungle
For years and years.

You like to see
River of boiling rock
Or giraffe motorway?
No? Got to catch boat?
Go well. Got any shiny discs
So Apeman can buy firewater?

Mainly for kids

Five Years Old

Five-year-olds dream of becoming giants —
Golden-bearded, striding around the map,
Gulping streams, munching sandwiches
Of crushed ice and white-hot anthracite
Between two slices of slate.
They sit on the edge of Salisbury Plain
Bawling huge songs across the counties
For ten days at a time,
Eating trees, cuddling carthorses,
Before stomping home to Windsor Castle.
They name clouds. They fall in love with buses,
They lick the stars, they are amazed by hoses,
They dance all the time because they don't think about
dancing . . .

They long to be allowed into the big good schools
Which will teach them to be giants with wings.

Giving Potatoes

STRONG MAN: Mashed potatoes cannot hurt you, darling
Mashed potatoes mean no harm
I have brought you mashed potatoes
From my mashed potato farm.

LADY: Take away your mashed potatoes
Leave them in the desert to dry
Take away your mashed potatoes —
You look like shepherd's pie.

BRASH MAN: A packet of chips, a packet of chips,
Wrapped in the *Daily Mail*,
Golden juicy and fried for a week
In the blubber of the Great White Whale.

LADY: Take away your fried potatoes
Use them to clean your ears
You can eat your fried potatoes
With birds-eye frozen tears.

OLD MAN: I have borne this baked potato
O'er the Generation Gap,
Pray accept this baked potato
Let me lay it in your heated lap.

LADY: Take away your baked potato
In your fusty musty van
Take away your baked potato
You potato-skinned old man.

FRENCHMAN: She rejected all potatoes
For a thousand nights and days
Till a Frenchman wooed and won her
With pommes de terre Lyonnaise.

LADY: Oh my corrugated lover
So creamy and so brown
Let us fly across to Lyons
And lay our tubers down.

41

To My Dog

This gentle beast
This golden beast
laid her long chin
along my wrist

and my wrist
is branded
with her love
and trust

and the salt of my cheek
is hers to lick
so long as I
or she shall last

Nature Poem

Skylark, what prompts your silver song
To fountain up and down the sky?

Beetles roast
With fleas on toast
And earthworm pie.

The Battle-Hymn of the
Ice-Cream Connoisseur

Mine eyes have seen the glory of
Pink Fudge Sundaes
I guzzle 'em on Saturdays and slurp on Mondays
I smuggle 'em to Chapel in my Grandma's undies
As my stomach rumbles on.

42

The Brave Heifer Stirk

(Based on a report from the *Craven Herald and Pioneer*
of July 17th, 1970.)

It is the thirteenth of July
In nineteen-seventy
Farmers pace Skipton marketplace
Unconscious of their jeopardy.

This heifer stirk in the Auction Mart
Is barely six months old.
But the brain beneath its yellow horns
Intones the words: 'I'll not be sold.'

The number card is all prepared
On the stirk's back to be stuck,
But the heifer stirk bursts from the ring.
Black mind in spate, bloodstream amok.

A score of farmers try to pass
Hairy white ropes around its neck
But the stirk upends the best of them
Then splatters down the beck.

It swaggers through King's Foundry Land
To Skipton Hospital,
Launches itself and swings across
The Leeds and Liverpool Canal.

Now Betty Thornton's trailer brings
The mother of the stirk to graze.
Monday night is armistice
But the dawn sets the stirk ablaze.

Tuesday: and the stirk marches
To its safe canal again.
It swims about two thousand yards
To disembark at Brewery Lane.

It slithers down to Eller Beck,
Then stamps downstream until
It stands in the black fifty yards
Of tunnel under Dewhurst's Mill.

For half an hour it drinks the dark,
Then re-emerges, thunderously.
Chased by the staff of the Auction Mart
And Skipton Town Constabulary.

In Gargrave Road it toys with cars
And jellifies the passers-by.
'O save us from this heifer stirk!'
The sad pedestrians cry.

Woodman Terrace becomes its lair....
A trap! This is a cul-de-sac!
Wheedlers advance with jailer's smiles
But the prongs of fury drive them back.

On the Girls' High School Tennis Courts
Pound those four havoc-wreaking feet.
Men sidle forward, one head is lowered,
Another charge, another mass retreat.

The foreman, Cyril Marshall, comes
From Skipton Auction Mart,
With Dave and Tommy Harrison,
Brothers no stirk shall ever part.

To stop a further charge is the attempt
Of Police Sergeant Michael Clemmett,
But, even helped by Constable O'Neil,
There is no way the law can stem it.

Now the stirk's mother is brought again
By trailer to the Tennis Court,
But though the stirk thrice mounts the ramp
It turns back with a rousing snort.

O, Marshall with his lasso all awhirl,
He cannot do the trick,
Nor Clemmett with a wooden form,
Nor O'Neil with a stick.

The Force means nothing to a stirk,
Freedom's its only rule,
It shoulders traffic all down Gargrave Road
To reach Ermysted's Grammar School.

Park Avenue, Coach Street, Broughton Road,
It takes at thumping rate,
Then stops beside a bungalow
On the Burnside Estate.

Four hours they've stalked that heifer stirk
While it played fast and loose.
Now Mr Longthorne, of the cattle-truck,
Secures it with his wily noose.

So here's a health to the heifer stirk
And to the Skipton steeplechase!
And may all who love their liberty
Run such a pretty race!

Watch Your Step — I'm Drenched

In Manchester there are a thousand puddles.
Bus-queue puddles poised on slanting paving stones,
Railway puddles slouching outside stations,
Cinema puddles in ambush at the exits,
Zebra-crossing puddles in dips of the dark stripes —
They lurk in the murk
Of the north-western evening
For the sake of their notorious joke,
Their only joke — to soak
The tights or trousers of the citizens.
Each splash and consequent curse is echoed by
One thousand dark Mancunian puddle chuckles.

In Manchester there lives the King of Puddles,
Master of Miniature Muck Lakes,
The Shah of Slosh, Splendifero of Splash,
Prince, Pasha and Pope of Puddledom.
Where? Somewhere. The rain-headed ruler
Lies doggo, incognito,
Disguised as an average, accidental mini-pool.
He is as scared as any other emperor,
For one night, all his soiled and soggy victims
Might storm his streets, assassination in their minds,
A thousand rolls of blotting paper in their hands,
And drink his shadowed, one-joke life away.

A Speck Speaks

About ten million years ago
I was a speck of rock in a vast black rock.
My address was:
Vast Black Rock,
Near Italy,
Twelve Metres Under
The Mediterranean Sea.

The other specks and I
Formed an impressive edifice —
Bulbously curving at the base
With rounded caves
And fun tunnels for the fish,
Romantically jagged at the top.

Life, for us specks, was uneventful —
One for all, welded together
In the cool, salty wet.
What more could specks
Expect?

Each year a few of us were lost,
Scrubbed from the edges of the rock
By the washerwoman waters
Which smoothed our base, whittled our cornices
And sharpened our pinnacles.
As the rock slowly shed skin-thin layers
It was my turn to be exposed
Among the packed grit of its surface,
(Near the tip of the fifty-ninth spire
From the end of the Eastern outcrop).

One day, it was a Wednesday I remember,
A scampi flicked me off my perch
Near the vast black rock's peak
And I was scurried down
Long corridors of currents
Until a wave caught me in its mouth

And spat me out on —
What?

A drying stretch
Of yellow, white, black, red and transparent specks,
Billions of particles,
Loosely organised in bumps and dips;
Quite unlike the tight hard group
Which I belonged to in the good old rock.
Heat banged down on us all day long.
Us? I turned to the speck next to me,
A lumpish red fellow who'd been washed off a brick.

'I'm new here,' I confessed,
'What are we supposed to be?'
He bellowed back —
(But the bellow of a speck
Is less than the whispering of ants) —
'We're grains now, grains of sand,
And this society is called Beach.'

'Beach?' I said, 'what are we grains supposed to do?'
'Just stray around, lie loose,
Go with the wind, go with the sea
And sink down when you're trodden on.'

'Don't know if I can manage that.
Used to belong to Vast Black Rock
And we all stuck together.'

'Give Beach a try,' said the red grain.
Well, there was no alternative.

Many eras later
I was just beginning to feel
Part of Beach, that slow-drifting,
Slow-shifting, casual community,
When I was shovelled up
With a ton of fellow-grains,
Hoisted into a lorry, shaken down a road,

Washed, sifted and poured in a machine
Hotter than the sunshine.

When they poured me out, life had changed again.
My mates and I swam in a molten river
Down into a mould.
White-hot we were, then red, then
Suddenly cold
And we found ourselves merged
Into a tall, circular tower,
Wide at the bottom, narrow at the top.
What's more, we'd all turned green as sea-weed,
Transparent green.
We had become a wine bottle.

In a few flashes of time
We'd been filled with wine,
Stoppered, labelled, bumped to a shop,
Stood in a window, sold, refrigerated,
Drained by English tourists,
Transmogrified into a lampstand.
Smashed by a four-year-old called Tarquin,
Swept up, chucked in the garbage, hauled away,
Dumped and bull-dozed into the sea.

Now the underwater years sandpaper away
My shield-shaped fragment of bottle.
So one day I shall be a single grain again,
A single grain of green, transparent glass.

When that day comes
I will transmit a sub-aquatic call
To all green specks of glass
Proposing that we form
A Vast Green Rock of Glass
Near Italy,
Twelve Metres Under
The Mediterranean Sea.
Should be pretty spectacular
In about ten million years.
All being well.

Deep Sherbet

deep sherbet
in a cardboard
cylinder
printed red
and yellow

used to poke
my liquorice
tube down through
the top and sucked

and when the sherbet
hit the spittle
on my palate —
that's when the fizz began

The Trumpeter of Ingleborough

January 22nd, about 7 p.m.
Too dark to see beyond the windows,
But I'm sure nobody has moved Ingleborough,
That pound-cake of rock, third highest point in Yorkshire
And (just my guess) the second heaviest.
Ingleborough must still be there.
But what else? What else is out
In the broad blackness tonight?

I guess. The first picture in my head
Is a man with a trumpet in his outstretched hand.
He stands, legs apart, black hair sprouting up from his
                                                    skull
On the flat top of Ingleborough.

I alter the picture to make it more likely.
A musician alone in a car, trumpet clutched.
But the car's moving, someone must be driving.
But the picture won't show the trumpeter driving
And he's alone, he seems to want to be alone.
I put him in a railway compartment.
He doesn't like it.
There's too much light in the compartment.
He blinks and blinks, even though I lower the lights,
And he's thinking somebody might come in
Any moment. That makes him anxious.

All right. I put him back in the car
But it keeps moving without a driver
And something is still wrong.
Something about him is sad.

So I take him back to where I found him
And he's berserk on Ingleborough,
Three times as large as life
And a huge moon makes his trumpet molten.
He laughs.
I ask his name.

Whether he hears me or not, he laughs,
And the name 'David' slides into my mind
And so I say 'David' but he takes no notice
But raises his trumpet to his mouth
And stretches his upper lip so I see each spike of stubble
And he blows.

First I hear nothing.
Then I hear the wind.
Then I hear a jet plane cut the sky.

I can see the trumpeter of Ingleborough
Without even closing my eyes.
And now he has stopped playing.

I try to see him sitting on a rock
But he won't sit down, he bounces up each time
And stands as I first saw him.

Silently I say: 'David',
And his head jerks forward
And he says, abruptly: 'Yes?'

And I say: 'What are you doing?'
And I wait. I try to hear him.
I think he says something, but very faintly.
It might be 'Living' or 'Dying' or 'Singing'.

I saw his boots just then.
They were strong, worn, dubbined brown,
Right for the rocks.
And I saw the flash of a beck
And a rock like a wedge of cheese
And then a cheese like a wedge of rock
And then a skinny tree and a deer,
But a foreign deer, African, maybe Okapi.

Now I've started seeing African things
Because of yesterday's TV travelogue . . .
A zebra rolling on his back in the dust.
Elephants shining in a river.

And when I look back to the mountain top in my head
It is bare. It shines.
The trumpeter has gone
Leaving only his shadow.

New Elephant Poems

The Galactic Pachyderm

The elephant stands
   among the stars
He jumps off
   Neptune
bounces off
   Mars
to adventures on
   Venus
while his children
   play
in the diamond jungles
   of the
Milky Way

Tinkling the Ivories

There was an elephant
   called Art Tatum
He played a piano
   whose teeth were human teeth

Non-event

If an elephant could meet a whale
their understanding would be huge
and they would love one another for ever

Bring Your Own Tankard

How to get permanently drunk in the jungle!
One pint of elephant's piss.

Pride

The elephant
is not proud of being an elephant
So why are we ashamed?

Good Tastes

The vilest furniture in this land
is an elephant's foot umbrella stand

Love Poem, Elephant Poem

Elephants are as amazing as love
but love is as amazing as elephants
Love is as amazing as elephants
but elephants are as amazing as love

Elephant Values

Nowhere in the world
is there an elephant bad enough
to make a career in advertising
or to play full-back for Leeds United

You Aren't What you Eat

The elephant
who's seldom flustered
despises calming food
like custard
Devouring curry
in a hurry
washed down with
a glass of mustard

Turn Turn Turn

There is a time for considering elephants
There is no time for not considering elephants

The infant elephant speaks:

I got a rusk
stuck on my tusk

Dumb Insolence

I'm big for ten years old
Maybe that's why they get at me

Teachers, parents, cops
Always getting at me

When they get at me

I don't hit em
They can do you for that

I don't swear at em
They can do you for that

I stick my hands in my pockets
And stare at them

And while I stare at them
I think about sick

They call it dumb insolence

They don't like it
But they can't do you for it

I've been done before
They say if I get done again

They'll put me in a home
So I do dumb insolence

One More Customer Satisfied

He staggered through the cities moaning for melons:
'Green melons streaked with yellow!
Yellow melons tinged with green!

'Don't try to fool me. They fooled me before
With tie-dyed green-and-yellow footballs
And the breasts of yellow women, green-tinted nipples . . .'

In his yellow rage and his green longing
He rolled himself into a melon-shaped heap of hopeless-
                                                    ness
Crying out: 'Melons! Bring out your melons!'

So they took a million melons to Cape Kennedy,
Scooped them out, filled them with green and yellow
                                        paint
And splattered them all over the bright side of the moon.

They adjusted his face so it faced the face of the moon
And they told him: 'There is your one true melon,
Your forever melon, your melon of melons.'
Now, fully grateful, he watches the melon rise,
The setting of the melon, the new melon and the full melon,
With a smile like a slice of melon in the green-and-yellow
                                            melon-light.

Beatrix is Three

At the top of the stairs
I ask for her hand. O.K.
She gives it to me.
How her fist fits my palm,
A bunch of consolation.
We take our time
Down the steep carpetway
As I wish silently
That the stairs were endless.

With Love

She is nearly eight.
Last night at eight o'clock
She looked at her whole life
And cried.

Second burst

Ceasefire

(Dedicated to the Medical Aid Committee for Vietnam, 36 Wellington Street, London WC2.)

The outside of my body was half-eaten
by fire which clings as tight as skin.
The fire has turned some of my skin
into black scab bits of roughness
and some pale bits smooth as plastic,
which no one dares touch
except me and the doctor.
Everyone who looks at me is scared.
That's not because I want to hurt people
but because so much of me
looks like the meat of a monster . . .

I was walking to the market.
Then I was screaming.
They found me screaming.
They put out the flames on my skin.
They laid me on a stretcher and I cried:
Not on my back!
So they turned me over and I cried:
Not on my front!

A doctor put a needle in my arm
and my mind melted
and I fell into a furnace of dreams of furnaces.

When I woke up I was in a white hospital.
Everything I wanted to say scared me
and I did not want to scare the others
in that white hospital,
so I said nothing, I cried as quietly as I could.

Months passed over my head
and bombers passed over my head
and people came and said they were my parents

and they found out the places on my face
where I could bear to be kissed.

And I pretended I could see them
but I couldn't really look out of my eyes
but only inwards, into my head
where the flames still clung and hurt, and talked.

And the flames said:
You are meat.
You are ugly meat.
Your body cannot grow to loveliness.
Nobody could love such ugly meat.
Only ugly meat could love such ugly meat.
Better be stewed for soup and eaten.

And months passed over my head
and bombers passed over my head
and the voices of the flames began to flicker
and I began to believe the people who said they were my
                                                    parents
were my parents.

And one day I threw myself forward
so that I sat up in bed, for the first time,
and hurled my arms around my mother,
and however the skin of my chest howled out in its pain
I held her, I held her, I held her
and knew she was my mother.
And I forgot that I was monster meat
and I knew she did not know that I was monster meat.

I held her, I held her.

And, sweet sun which blesses all the world —
all the flames faded.
The flames of my skin
and the flames inside my head —
all the flames faded
and I was flooded
with love for my mother

who did not know
that I was monster meat.

And so, in the love-flood, I let go of my mother
and fell back upon my pillow
and I rolled my head to the left side
and I saw a child, or it might have been an old man,
eating his rice with his only arm
and I rolled my head to the right side
and saw another child, or she might have been an old
                                                    woman,
being fed through the arm from a tube from a red bottle —
and I loved them, and, flooded with love
I started to sing
the song of the game I used to play with my friends
in the long-ago days before the flames came:

> One, one, bounce the ball,
> Once for the sandal-maker,
> Two, two, bounce the ball,
> Twice for the fishermen on the river.
> Three, three, bounce the ball,
> Three times for your golden lover —

And had to stop singing.
Throat choked with vomit.

And then the flames exploded again all over my skin
and then the flames exploded again inside my head
and I burned, sweet sun, sweet mother, I burned.

> Sweet sun, which blesses all the world,
> this was one of the people of Vietnam.
> Make him or her whatever age you like —
> he or she is dead.

> The one-armed man or boy survives.
> The woman or girl
> whose body needs a change of blood each day
> survives.

I suppose we love each other.
We're stupid if we don't.

We have a choice —
Either to choke to death on our own vomit
or to become one
with the sweet sun, which blesses all the world.

Celia Celia

When I am sad and weary
When I think all hope has gone
When I walk along High Holborn
I think of you with nothing on

Footnotes on Celia Celia

Used to slouch along High Holborn
in my gruesome solo lunch-hours.
It was entirely lined
with Gothick insurance offices
except for one oblong block of a shop
called Gamages,
where, once,
drunk, on Christmas Eve,
I bought myself a battery-operated Japanese pig
with a chef's hat on top of his head
and a metal stove which lit up red
and the pig moved a frying pan up and down with his
hand
and tossed a plastic fried egg into the air
and caught it again the other way up
and then tossed it and caught it again and again
all the time emitting squeals of excitement
through a series of holes in the top of his head —

but apart from that . . . I want to forget High Holborn.

Lady Macbeth in the Saloon Bar Afterwards

It was all going surprisingly well —
Our first school matinee and we'd got up to
My sleepwalking scene with the minimum of titters . . .
Right, enter me, somnambulistically.
One deep sigh. Then some lout tosses
A banana on to the forestage.
It got a round? Darling, it got a thunderstorm!
Of course, we carried on, but suddenly
We had a panto audience
Yelling out: 'Look out! He's behind you!'
Murders, battles, Birnham Wood, great poetry -
All reduced to mockery.
The Bard upstaged by a banana.
Afterwards we had a flaming row in the Grenville
About just who should have removed it
And just when —
One of the servants, obviously.
And ever since, at every performance:
Enter myself in those exquisite ribbons
And — plomp — a new out-front banana.
Well, yes, it does affect *all* our performances
But actually, *they* seem to love it.
And how, now Ben's in Canada
Doling out Wesker to the Eskimos,
Can we decide who *exits with banana*?
You can't expect me to parade down there,
Do a sort of boob-baring curtsey and announce:
'Is this a banana that I see before me?'
Anyway, darling, we may have egg on our faces —
But we've got a hit on our hands.

The Ballad of Sally Hit-and-Run

A train pulls into town and a woman jumps down
Her leathers are shining and her eyes are shining
With the body of a goddess and the cool of a nun
Everywhere she goes they call her Sally Hit-and-Run.

She moves down the street with a shuffle and a beat
Of her feet on the concrete — she's a creature
With senses that respond to every sound in town
And a hit-and-run habit when the sun goes down.

Sally Hit-and-Run on a barstool perch
Glances round the bar like a rector in church
Then she points one finger like a sensitive gun
And another guy topples to Sally Hit-and-Run.

Holiday Inn, Room three hundred and three,
Sally got him wrapped around the colour TV!
She shakes him and she bangs him like a tambourine,
Then she spreads him on the carpet like margarine.

Up comes the dawn — Sally's gone like a dream
Riding Inter-City drinking coffee and cream
Guy's left counting up the things he's done
Trying to give his goodness to Sally Hit-and-Run.

What Men Fear in Women

is as camouflaged
as a group of cougars
lying, perhaps,
among the spots of light and shadow
below a hot, astonishing tree

What Men Fear in Other Men

is as obvious
as the shining photographs
and cross-section diagrams
in a brochure provided,
with a smile, by a car salesman

English Scene

You sit at a table with two other men

Your left wrist slants in front of your throat
Your right incisors chew the nail of your left little
                                        finger
Your right index fingernail ploughs across the grain of
                                        the tabletop

You are nervous, obviously

You are right to be nervous, obviously

The man on one side of you has less money than you
He wants your money

The man on the other side of you has more money than
                                        you
He wants your money

Your left arm protects your throat
They usually go for the throat

A Warning

If you keep two angels in a cage
They will eat each other to death

My Dog Eats Nuts Too

(Chekhov: *The Cherry Orchard*)

The sperm bank manager shoved me up against the rail
he levelled his gamma ray at my adventure tail
he said I've followed you through fire and flood and firkin
And you'd better explain just what you think you're
working

I said:
I'm not a motivational expert you'd better suppose
but the trouble is my brain is a long way behind my nose
I believe in saluting the animals, my motto is dig and
have done,
but I spend all my problemofleisure grabbing lots of
chinese fun

having chinese fun
having chinese fun
you don't need a mantelpiece
when you're having chinese fun

He said:
you're chewing something terrible, show us your
expectoration,
so I banged the spittoon with western civilization
he clamped me with his grabbers and shook me till my
steeple rung
tell me what's so special he said about chinese fun

having chinese fun
having chinese fun
happy as the hebrides
when I'm having chinese fun

I said:
it moves like a leopard on ice cubes
glows like hot molasses
it's a shady bank by the old gulf stream

and there's masses and masses and masses for the masses
giggles every time that it tries to be sensible
striped with sex well it's highly reprehensible
but I'll bring you a cut of it only costs a dollar a ton
and you'll feel like a Zen Gun once you've tasted chinese
fun

having chinese fun
having chinese fun
take the moon and rub it all over the surface of the sun
and you'll turn in your badge
when you've had some chinese fun

He tried it.
He liked it.
He said: thank you.

A Ballad of Human Nature

The Buddha sat on a banana crate
Sunning his mind in the shade,
Trying to imagine Aggressive,
Trying to imagine Afraid.

A man staggered up to the Buddha,
He was horrified and thin.
He was hacking with a knife at his body,
Paring his own skin.

The Buddha said: 'Be kind to yourself.'
The thin man lowered his knife;
Then he said, as his blood ran into the earth:
'Where've you been all your life?

'You know, you can't change human nature just like
           that.
I once saw it proved in a book by a scientist's rat.
We're jellies shaking with atavistic greed.
You can't change human nature — you may as well bleed.'

To the Organizers of a Poetry Reading by Hugh Macdiarmid

You chose the wrong place —
A neutral room with tawny blinds pulled down.
You pulled the wrong audience —
The gabbiest cultural bureaucrats in town.
You picked the wrong poet —
Too clever too daft too great for you to deserve his
                                        spittle
And you brought the wrong whisky
And you only bought him half a bottle.

Divide and Rule for as Long as you can

Glasgow.
Trade Unionists march through the Square
Towards the City Chambers.

Police. Police. Police.

And in the streets leading off the Square —
Scottish soldiers with rifles.
Live ammunition.
They may be ordered to shoot into the crowd.

And behind the Scottish soldiers —
English soldiers with rifles.
Live ammunition.
If the Scottish soldiers refuse to shoot into the crowd
The English soldiers will be ordered
To shoot the Scottish soldiers

Oh, but that was long ago.

That was in the future.

The Open Savage

the open savage
enters a roomful of coded conversation
the open savage
hides underneath himself

the open savage
is invaded by visions
the open savage
sings embarrassingly

the open savage
attends a logical dissection of the universe
the open savage
weeps as he throws baked beans at the platform

the open savage
does not explain himself
the open savage
is himself

the open savage
is accused of being open
the open savage
smiles like a jar of honey with no lid

Now we are Sick

Christopher
       Robin
            goes
                hippety
immigrants   hoppety
       bring down
             the value of
                  property

And some Lemonade too

Drinking gin eating curry
That's my second favourite game
Begin feeling hollow
Then you sip and swallow
Till they start to taste about the same
Well gin got a bite
Curry got a burn
Try to teach your tongue to take them in turn
Drinking gin eating curry
Shoobi doobi wah wah

Drinking gin eating curry
Feeling my way to my ease
When the curry was dead
The gin hit my head
Till I fell down on my knees
Curry's ambrosia
Gin is the elixir
I am the champion concrete-mixer
Eating gin drinking curry
Shoobi doobi wah wah

Drinking gin eating curry
Gulped down all my trouble
Spent a magical sleep
In a happy old heap
And woke up with chutney-flavour alcohol stubble
Took a look at heaven
Took a look at hell
Reckoned I fancied them equally well
Sinking gin and beating curry
Wah wah shoobi doobi wah wah wah

Toy Stone

I dived and found it.

A wedge of stone,
Grey mixed with the mauve
Of sky before snow.
Flakes of crystal
Shining among its mineral clouds.

Now and again I look at the stone,
Convert it into the relief map
Of a nude island or the night sky.
Or use it as a racquet
For bouncing light into my eyes.

Today I took it with my eyes shut.
Turning the stone between my hands
I learned
That it shares the shape and weight
Of a small pistol.

Now it has a barrel,
A chamber and a butt.
Held by the barrel, it could be used
To bash almost anything to death.

Stone-shine is in my head,
But so is the killing weight of the stone.

Toy stone, weapon stone.
I will keep it.

Night Lines in a Peaceful Farmhouse

truth is
exactly the same size as the universe
and my eyes are narrow

i stare at one of my fingernails
its mass is pink
its edge is blue with coke-dust
it grows on a warm well-nourished hand

i look up and suck smoke
the windows are black

people are being killed

the first time i met a girl called Helen
she told me
'money is the basis of life'
the second time i met her she said
'money is the basis of life'

people are being killed

i stare at those four words
typed in black
they are true words
but they do not bleed
and die and rot

commonplace cruelty
timetable cruelty

i haven't seen much of the world
but i've seen enough

i have known more horror in half an hour
than i shall ever have the skill to tell

my right hand soothes my left hand

i have known more beauty in half a minute
than i shall ever have the skill to tell

i make a fond small smile
remembering gentleness in many cities

so many good people

and people are being killed

Two Paintings by Manuel Mendive

1
The road is a snake guarded by vultures
A man on white crutches
hauls a wagonload of corpses.
He is crying blood.

2
God sits creating a bright halo of birds.
He sits on a mountain of dark people
who are impaled by everyday nails.

Royal Whodunnit

after the Coronation
they found upon the Throne
    a new-laid turd
    as hard as stone

Many Many Many Mansions

(An ode on the occasion of the completion of an inter-denominational Chaplaincy Centre at the University of Lancaster.)

This house was built for God.
It looks good.

'You can sit on the toilet and cook your dinner, and you don't have to stretch out at all,' a pregnant woman told us.

Another house for God,
In case he visits Lancaster University.

He had come home from work to find his flat flooded with sewage overflowing from upstairs.

Every new house for God
Is a joke by the rich against the poor.

'If my baby lives, the welfare may give me a place with two bedrooms. If it dies, I'll have to stay here.'

Every new house for God
Is blasphemy against humanity.

Christians and others, when you need to pray,
Go to the kitchens of the slums,
Kneel to the mothers of the slums,
Pray to the children of the slums.
The people of the slums will answer your prayers.

What the Mermaid Told Me

(For the Fiftieth Anniversary of the British Broadcasting
Corporation.)

*(Every sentence in the middle section of the piece was
broadcast by BBC TV during the period July 13th —
August 12th, 1972).*

Strapped on my aqualung and flippered my way
To the bed of the electric ocean.
The water was flickering white and grey
And thick as calamine lotion.
Groped along the rocks till my hand came to rest
On the luke-warm pudding of a mermaid's breast.
She was British, broad, corporate and fiftyish
With a hint of aristocracy
Her top was woman and her arse was fish
And this is what she said to me:

'How dangerous are these cable cars?
We have a lot of fun on this show.
When is all this killing going to stop?
I think they deserve some applause, don't you?

'We are very environment-conscious.
This is like a bloody Xmas grotto.
What if everyone else refused to obey
The laws of which they don't approve?

'What does Muswell Hill mean to you?
Will the ceasefire stick?
He was not the man to embarrass the police.
I think they deserve some applause, don't you?

'I came to an arrangement with him
To come up with 40 million dollars.
When I sing my songs you can't sit still,
Your big toe shoot up in your boot.

'If only women could get on with women
Like men get on with men.
It's lovely for me to be sitting
In a seat like this again.

'Just in one day our lives were crushed.
I don't want to be an old curmudgeon.
Are the five senses enough any more?
I think they deserve some applause, don't you?

'You're doing to this country what Hitler failed
                                                to do.
Has he been the victim of a personal witch-hunt?
He makes no bones about carrying the can
For Rio Tinto Zinc.

'There is going to be a very high attrition rate
In this field of 26 starters,
Look all around, there's nothing but blue skies.
We'll kill 'em all or get back into Cambodia.

'I've had people who've had conversion experiences
Following leucotomy.
You can never be certain of anything in Ireland
I think they deserve some applause, don't you?

'British public life is singularly free from any taint
of corruption at all.
Our towns are almost ready to be destroyed, they
    are uninhabitable, they are completely contrary to
    human life
The British found it necessary to intervene to protect
    their interests.
There are so few young women in Highbury who are
    in any way suitable
What has become of your traditional British phlegm
    and common sense?
We're only giving the public what they want.
I think they deserve some applause, don't you?'

The mermaid was ten thousand times as heavy as me
And the scales of her tail were moulting.
But since she was the hottest thing in the sea
She was also the least revolting.
I proposed a little sexual action
And she smiled (which was mostly gaps),
And she wriggled her satisfaction
As she whispered to me: 'Perhaps.'

Confession

Of course I've been corrupted by publicity
A friendly journalist once likened me to Bogart
And I took to exposing my upper teeth when I smiled at
enemies

Several years later I was in a theatre
At the same time as Lauren Bacall
And she was so beautiful I could only look at her for
two seconds

And that was enough,
Sam, that was plenty.

One Question about Amsterdam

Of course it all looked good in the good light.
(Even the grandmother prostitute
Who leaned too far over her window-sill
As she picked her nose and ate it
And only stopped, with the guiltiest
Guilty start I've ever seen,
When she saw I was looking.)
Of course it all looked good,
But, since I was suspicious even in the womb,
And, as it turns out, rightly suspicious,
Forgive me, Hans, one miniature complaint.

I didn't see a single Eskimo in Amsterdam.
Everything else, yes, but no Eskimos.
Not one candle-chewing, wife-lending,
Blubber-loving igloo freak
Of an ice-hole fishing, polar bear-clobbering Nanook.
Throughout the tranquilizing waterways,
Throughout the bumping wet of the harbour —
Not one bloody kayak.

Where are the eskimos of Amsterdam?
Where are the eskimos of Amsterdam?
Where are the eskimos of Amsterdam?

Discovery

Unpopular, Tibetan and four foot two,
He ran an underground cocktail bar
Near the pit-face of a Congolese coal-mine.
Nobody would listen to his stories
So he scribbled them on the backs of beer-mats,
One sentence on each mat.
Because he hated coal
He wrote, mostly, about the sea.

Years later two critics from Cambridge
Spent their honeymoon at the same colliery.
They discovered a black chamber
Empty but for a hundred thousand beer-mats.

After years of beer-mat shuffling and transcription
The critics published the text
As The Fictional Works of Joseph Conrad.

Three cheers for the critics!
Three cheers for Cambridge!
Where would Joseph Conrad be without them?
Down the mine.

Where be Joseph Conrad?
Two hundred yards down in the same Congolese pit,
Serving mint juleps to the husky miners,
Speaking when he is spoken to.

A Tourist Guide to England

£ Welcome to England!
England is a happy country.

£ Here is a happy English businessman.
Hating his money, he spends it all
On bibles for Cambodia
And a charity to preserve
The Indian Cobra from extinction.

£ I'm sorry you can't see our happy coal-miners.
Listen hard and you can hear them
Singing Welsh hymns far underground.
Oh. The singing seems to have stopped.

£ No, that is not Saint Francis of Assisi.
That is a happy English policeman.

£ Here is a happy black man.
No, it is not illegal to be black. Not yet.

£ Here are the slums.
They are preserved as a tourist attraction.
Here is a happy slum-dweller.
Hello, slum-dweller!
No, his answer is impossible to translate.

£ Here are some happy English schoolchildren.
See John. See Susan. See Mike.
They are studying for their examinations.
Study, children, study!
John will get his O-Levels
And an O-Level job and an O-Level house and an
                                    O-Level wife.
Susan will get her A-Levels
And an A-Level job and an A-Level house and an
                                    A-Level husband.
Mike will fail.

£ Here are some happy English soldiers.
  They are going to make the Irish happy.

£ No, please understand.
  We understand the Irish
  Because we've been sending soldiers to Ireland
  For hundreds and hundreds of years.

£ First we tried to educate them
  With religion, famine and swords.
  But the Irish were slow to learn.

£ Then we tried to educate them
  With reason, poverty and unemployment.
  They became silent, sullen, violent.

£ So now we are trying to educate them
  With truncheons, gas, rubber bullets,
  Steel bullets, internment and torture.
  We are trying to teach the Irish

  To be as happy as us.

£ So please understand us
  And if your country
  Should be forced to educate
  Another country in the same way,
  Or your own citizens in the same way —
  We will try to understand you.

Ode to the Sponsors of the British Appeal Committee of Europalia '73

(or: Who's Who in International Daylight Robbery)

O Lord Adeane, Lord Aldington
Sir Cyril Kleinwort, Kleinwort Benson,
    Intercede for us.
O ICI O Rio Tinto Zinc
    Colonize us in our unworthiness.
O Sir Paul Chambers, KBE,
    In our hour of need.
O Rothschild and Sons, Phoenix Assurance,
Sir Martin Wilkinson, The Stock Exchange,
The Honourable Sir Marcus Sieff of Marks and Spencer
    Shower thy blessings.
O Maxwell Joseph, Watney Mann,
British American Tobacco Co.
    Deliver us from cancer.
O Sotheby's, EMI, Metal Box Company,
    Do what thou wilt with us,
O General Fire and Life Assurance,
    Reassure and interfere with us.
O Whitbreads, Sidney Spiro, Slough Estates,
    Won't you slip it to us?
O Hon John Baring, Baring Foundation,
Instone Bloomfield of Oddeninos,
    Really do it to us.
O British Petroleum, O Guinness, Bank of England,
    Come on, won't you sock it to us?
O Viscount Harcourt, O Sir Jack Lyons,
Colonel J D Fitzjohn, Sir Eric Roll, Lord Goodman
And others too powerful to mention —
    I mean, really stick it up us.
Sir Don Ryder, ride us.
Sir Max Rayne, rain upon us.
Sir Brian Mountain, mount upon us —

    I see your names
    Written in flames.

Sorry Bout That

Truth is a diamond
A diamond is hard
You don't exist
Without a Barclaycard

Sorry bout that
Sorry bout that
Even South African cops
Do the sorry bout that

They showed me the world and said:
What do you think?
I said: half about women
And half about drink

And I'm sorry bout that
Sorry bout that
Mother, I need that booze
And I'm sorry bout that

If you cut your conscience
Into Kennomeat chunks
You can get elected
To the House of Drunks

Sorry bout that
Sorry bout that
You'll never have to think again
And I'm sorry bout that

You can do the Skull
Or the Diplomat
But I do a dance called
The Sorry Bout That

Do the Mighty Whitey
Or the Landlord Rat

But I'll keep grooving to
The Sorry Bout That

Sorry bout that
Sorry bout that
They make me dance with pistols and ten to one
I'm sorry bout that

I saw Money walking
Down the road
Claws like an eagle
And a face like a toad

Well I know your name baby
Seen you before
Slapping on your make-up
For the Third World War

Sorry bout that
Sorry bout that
Someone set the world on fire
And I'm sorry bout that

Victor Jara of Chile

(This ballad may be sung to the tune of Woody Guthrie's
Dear Mrs. Roosevelt.)

Victor Jara of Chile
Lived like a shooting star
He fought for the people of Chile
With his songs and his guitar

And his hands were gentle
His hands were strong

Victor Jara was a peasant
Worked from a few years old
He sat upon his father's plough
And watched the earth unfold

And his hands were gentle
His hands were strong

When the neighbours had a wedding
Or one of their children died
His mother sang all night for them
With Victor by her side

And his hands were gentle
His hands were strong

He grew to be a fighter
Against the people's wrongs
He listened to their grief and joy
And turned them into songs

And his hands were gentle
His hands were strong

He sang about the copper miners
And those who work the land
He sang about the factory workers
And they knew he was their man

And his hands were gentle
His hands were strong

He campaigned for Allende
Working night and day
He sang: take hold of your brother's hand
The future begins today

And his hands were gentle
His hands were strong

The bloody generals seized Chile
They arrested Victor then
They caged him in a stadium
With five thousand frightened men

And his hands were gentle
His hands were strong

Victor stood in the stadium
His voice was brave and strong
He sang for his fellow-prisoners
Till the guards cut short his song

And his hands were gentle
His hands were strong

They broke the bones in both his hands
They beat his lovely head
They tore him with electric shocks
After two long days of torture they shot him dead

And his hands were gentle
His hands were strong

And now the Generals rule Chile
And the British have their thanks
For they rule with Hawker Hunters
And they rule with Chieftain tanks

And his hands were gentle
His hands were strong

Victor Jara of Chile
Lived like a shooting star
He fought for the people of Chile
With his songs and his guitar

And his hands were gentle
His hands were strong